STEAM JOB? DREAM JOB!

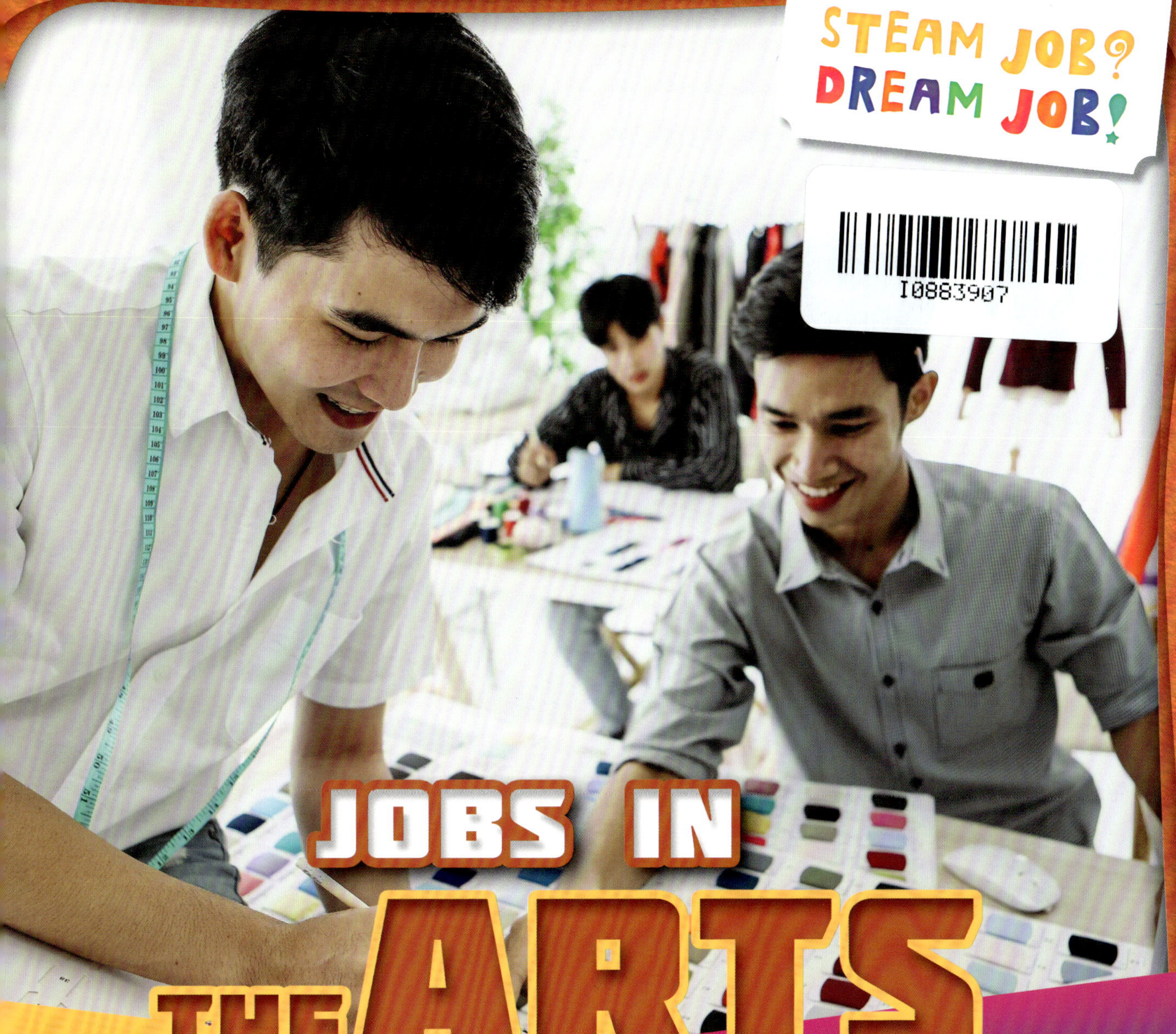

JOBS IN THE ARTS

By Bethany Latham

KidHaven PUBLISHING

Published in 2026 by
KidHaven Publishing, an Imprint of
Greenhaven Publishing, LLC
2544 Clinton St., Buffalo, NY 14224

Written by: Bethany Latham
Edited by: Rebecca Phillips-Bartlett
Designed by: Rob Delph

Cataloging-in-Publication Data

Names: Latham, Bethany.
Title: Jobs in the arts / Bethany Latham.
Description: Buffalo, NY : KidHaven Publishing, 2026. | Series: STEAM job? Dream job! | Includes glossary and index.
Identifiers: ISBN 9781534552128 (pbk.) | ISBN 9781534552135 (library bound) | ISBN 9781534552142 (ebook)
Subjects: LCSH: Cultural industries--Vocational guidance--Juvenile literature. | Arts--Vocational guidance--Juvenile literature
Classification: LCC HD9999.C9472 L384 2026 | DDC 700.23--dc23

Printed in China

CPSIA compliance information: Batch #QW26KH: For further information contact Greenhaven Publishing LLC at 1-844-317-7404.

Please visit our website, www.greenhavenpublishing.com. For a free color catalog of all our high-quality books, call toll free 1-844-317-7404 or fax 1-844-317-7405.

Find us on

IMAGE CREDITS

Images courtesy of Shutterstock.com, unless otherwise stated.

Cover – Pavlo S, YamabikaY, Bangkok Click Studio, GoodStudio, David Lugasi. 2–3 – Viktor Gladkov, metamorworks, GoodStudio. 4–5 – PeopleImages.com - Yuri A, cineuno, BigPixel Photo, Pressmaster, Monkey Business Images, ST.art. 6–7 – Viktor Gladkov, GoodStudio, PeopleImages.com - Yuri A. 8–9 – DC Studio, LightField Studios, David Lugasi. 10–11 – Frame Stock Footage, Mariana_Rusanovschi. 12–13 – Jorge Elizaquibel, Winter Summer Media, Ruangdej Chulert. 14–15 – SeventyFour, amarklc. 16–17 – Frame Stock Footage, Iryna Imago, Julia Babii. 18–19 – Wayhome Studio, Prostock-studio, Thomas Pajot. 20–21 – Gorodenkoff, metamorworks, fiestachka. 22–23 – guys_who_shoot, Krakenimages.com, riabchevskii. 24 – David Lugasi, Ruangdej Chulert. Vectors used throughout – Pavlo S, YamabikaY.

CONTENTS

Words that look like **this** can be found in the glossary on page 24.

ALL ABOUT STEAM

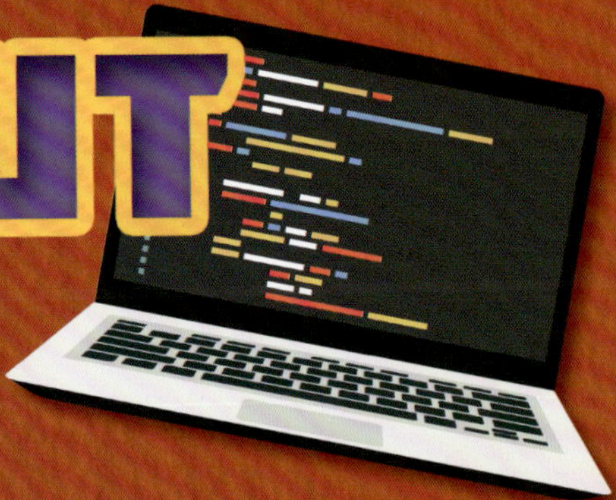

There are so many amazing **careers**. Have you thought about what you want to do when you grow up? Many jobs use skills you learn in STEAM classes—science, technology, engineering, the arts, and math.

There are many different STEAM careers. You could go into areas such as farming, archaeology, and movies. STEAM subjects share many of the same skills. Skills in one subject could help you in another.

ALL ABOUT THE ARTS

The arts include more than just drawing and painting. They include all the ways people express themselves creatively. This can include writing, music, movies, and more.

THE ARTS OFTEN DEAL WITH STORYTELLING. IF YOU LOVE STORIES, A JOB IN THE ARTS MIGHT BE YOUR DREAM JOB!

The arts are about people. Through art, people can share how they feel about things. The arts are all about **connecting** with others. There are many different careers in the arts.

JOURNALIST

Journalists tell people about the news and other events happening in the world. They work in many different places. Journalists may write for newspapers or magazines, talk on television, or work online.

JOURNALISTS ARE SOMETIMES CALLED REPORTERS.

Many journalists only report on one topic. They might report on sports, food, or other countries. Journalists **interview** people to get information, or facts. They need very good listening skills. Journalists also need to be truthful.

ARCHAEOLOGIST

Archaeologists study human history. They look at objects and writing from the past. Archaeologists also take part in digs. This involves digging in carefully chosen spots to find **artifacts**.

Many archaeologists become **specialists** in one historical time, such as the Stone Age. Other archaeologists specialize in one place. Egyptologists focus on the history of ancient Egypt in Africa.

VIDEOGRAPHER

Videographers film video footage. They might film television ads, news stories, or music videos. Some videographers film events such as weddings. Once they have filmed everything, videographers often **edit** the footage together.

BE INSPIRED!

WHEN YOU WATCH TELEVISION, THINK ABOUT HOW THEY TELL THE STORY.

Some videographers are freelancers, which means they work for themselves. Other videographers work for big companies or studios. Videographers need experience working with filming **equipment** and computers. They also need good storytelling skills.

CONSERVATOR

Conservators look after and repair artifacts, artwork, and buildings. There are two types of conservation. Remedial conservation involves fixing objects. Preventative conservation tries to stop objects from getting damaged in the first place.

CONSERVATORS MIGHT FOCUS ON ONE TYPE OF CONSERVATION OR BOTH.

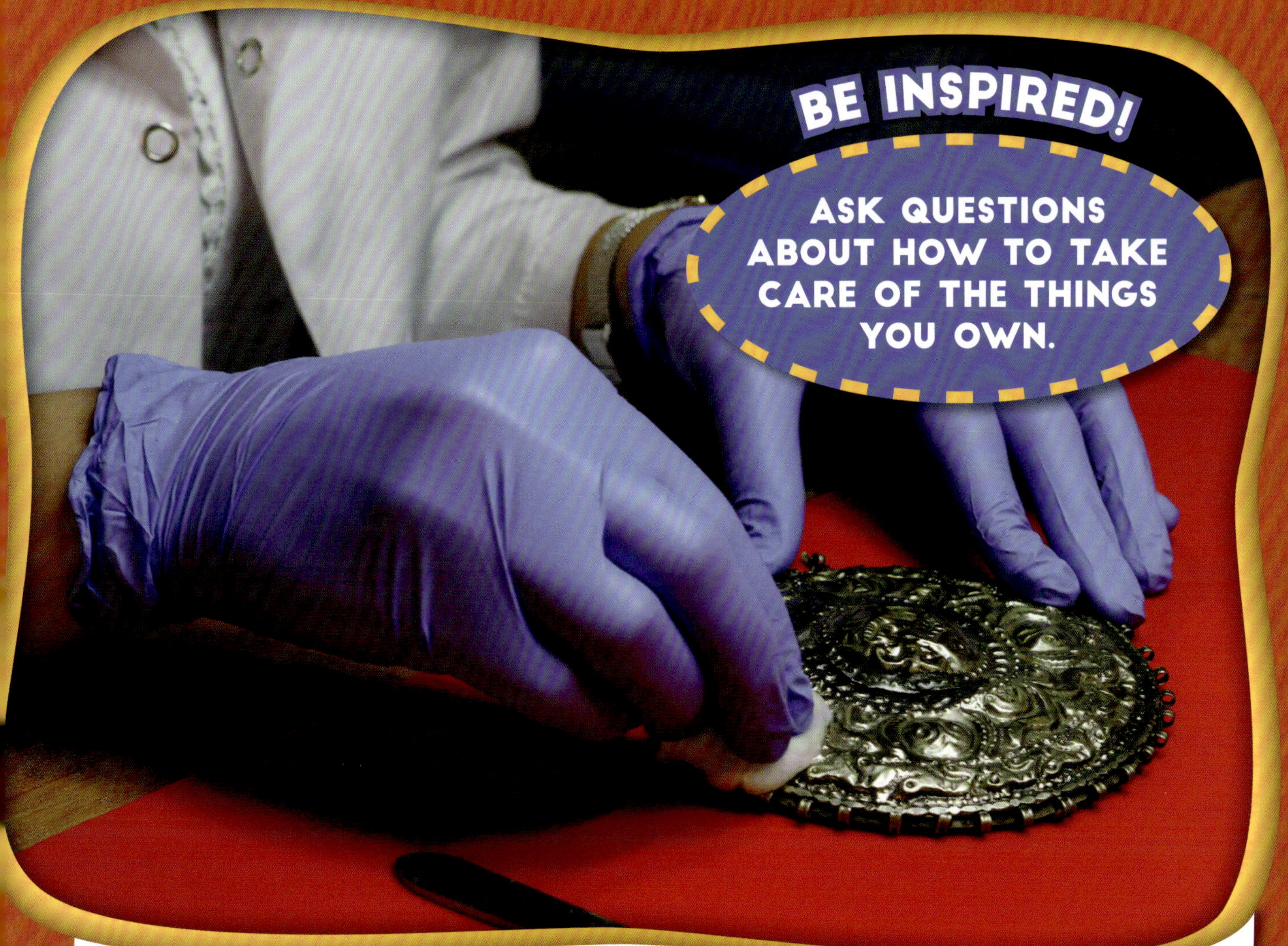

Some conservators work in museums or libraries. Others work in historical houses. Many conservators specialize in one thing, such as **textiles**, paintings, or glass. Conservators need special knowledge and training.

ANIMATOR

STOP MOTION ANIMATORS TAKE HUNDREDS OF PHOTOS OF REAL MODELS.

Animators are artists. They create images that look like they are moving when they are played one after another very quickly. Some animation is hand-drawn. Other animation is done on computers.

Animators usually work in big teams at animation studios. They work in television, movies, video games, and more. Animators need art and technology skills. They must know how to tell a good story through images.

BE INSPIRED!

PRACTICE CREATING STORIES THROUGH DRAWINGS. ASK AN ADULT ABOUT FLIPBOOKS!

INTERIOR DESIGNER

Interior designers plan how an inside space will look. They decide where all the furniture goes and how the space is **decorated**. Interior designers work in homes, offices, and public spaces.

Interior designers need to understand how color can make a space feel. Interior designers must talk to their **clients** to understand what they need or want, so they need good listening skills.

ACTOR

Actors tell stories by playing characters. They use their bodies and voices to bring the characters to life. Actors might perform in movies, on television, on the stage, or in voice-over work such as cartoons.

SOME ACTORS SING AND DANCE. THEY MIGHT PERFORM IN MUSICALS.

Actors often do research and learn new skills to play different characters. Many actors go to acting school. They learn how to make their characters feel real. Actors need to do a lot of practice.

THE POWER OF STEAM

We have looked at just a few of the arts careers you could have. There are many more. The arts are always changing. New ideas are being created all the time.

BE INSPIRED!

WHICH ARTS CAREER SOUNDS MOST EXCITING TO YOU?

If you enjoy the arts, there are many things you can do when you grow up. You can bring people joy through creativity. Your school STEAM subjects will give you all the skills you need.

GLOSSARY

ARTIFACTS objects that were made in the past

CAREERS job areas that can be worked in for a large amount of a person's life

CLIENTS customers who are paying for a service

CONNECTING joining or bringing together

DECORATED when a space is painted or has things added to it to make it look nicer

EDIT to put video footage together to make a complete video or story

EQUIPMENT items that are needed to complete a certain job

INTERVIEW to ask a person questions to find out more about them or a another topic

SPECIALISTS people who focus on a particular subject or skill

TEXTILES fabric or cloth made by hand or on a machine

INDEX